The Type a Thing

The Type a Thing

Tom Kraft

Left Hand Books

The publisher and the author gratefully acknowledge the John W. and Clara C. Higgins Foundation for its generous support in the funding of this book.

The author would like to thank his family and friends for their love and support. Particular thanks to Rodney Hill, Jeremy Sigler and Bryan McHugh for their encouragement and aid.

Designed by Bryan McHugh.

Distributed by SPD, Berkeley, CA.
Left Hand Books website: lefthandbooks.com

ISBN 1-880516-29-2

Manufactured in the United States of America.

May this help free all who see and hear it.

Can dogs
argue
injustices

Dogs in a vise,
and a wood saw
can saw an anatomy
of dog

Such as you never saw.

If it yowls
shut the eyelid on a bad dream,
Let not the snarls take,
With its virus in you
You are immune.

What hounds
you means to.
Not all woodsawyers
grow animal.

from A, *Louis Zukofsky*

The Type a Thing

A

Tire of a roving car of danger.
Next stall a blank cave
along the curve dream of a holy future.
X and its approaching
Y contain derangements havens switch
back normal. Colors blim
to time tinkertoys cannot emit.
Objects again come and
sonnets angle a nebulous
dot on the periphery
that gridded magic tone.
All boing easy out that word and word
next across and up to next.
A manual cranking
above a silted river arm
lairs out a flock to think again.
Frisk a shiver yes and no
to offer a piece where
functions dot dash asymptotes:

this X breeds the shaken reactor love.
Drivel a birth flew up a lip it
then lists and feathers.
Over the origin
non persona aqua circle area
concentric pupil growth down there
poll and pool
a concord earth to grieve the land of planes.

B

A level one want of a
public boring nothing.

Ice cream taste no body
but fuck thought see-saws.

Woe a sound calliope farther

further than an organ can
toot to total it.

Breathe and breath again
froze again to noon.

Toothy ego of his Cantos
square mouth anger remember

Osiris or smiles fool through

America run tap dictaphone
or an inch toot einen sums it

too much up to it.

C

Doo-doo and daa-daa calculus
change dipthong

the castanet sequences

ears to wharf for war or
shine through

a kilt though laugh
a declarative war of

red boom
and rat-a-tat taters.

Snare thee a loop
pin hole up close the leg that up

memory stein raised
and strike a toast

boat

snakes wound blue
contusions around by thinking up Uniform Street.

No tread on it.
Downed on a bike so fast runs out

to love. Dora about to
never skid again if

her crying never is thought
again.

A mother never
to her Mary prayers to

engage to give up a kind
thought of

never collating but only get constant time

a better kind of emotion.
Occur and it occurs given over

to ask over the news again is not

a b-c glider floating cross.
The sign out the third dimension the fifth dimension.

Not that one
but one that counts accords

up to three
two there never to close those

curves who count to it:
color claims in an attuned driftwood

tune to catapult
antennae song difficultly

river across

real time causes real time

to be a given to a theorem.

Or stone skipper.

D

In the fourth quadrant
true X is positive
and Y is negative.

Found slant
of two dots make line slope.

Lost mouth a disc a
mountain maintained
a snapped blanket peak.

Whoee of
embracing language there!

Pet a fun dog for real!

A true line cannot stay
that quadrant exclusively.

Ironically half a hyperbola can.

A quartic can’t
but beautiful math can
emote like any
drawing across quadrature:

Candy climbs
his red
bark roving
iactae puerae.

Or:

Any Warhol can
hold sight

up loosely group
air break

bread wise roof dissolve.

I love you a mind
game to the young.

To the old the
game is young.

To a fawn leaps
articulate mirrors

a braid a bulb departs to
a bright bust caroming Lethe

left star surfacing.

E

Marinetti was
not that dump.

Marinetti was a doll up there.
See

write paint really
write people. I broke Sistine

houses of paper
and ink to arc figura 17.

Already an image number
so I enter this one in.

Figs found at June's end
smith string straight from a cube.

I tire and hope for striving.

People borne by striving

orf thyme to kink more those horns for astra.

Hinder squall who think
got hovered

banks these two dimensions.

And counter rhyme time in a helix
modo of all seen and unseen.

Molting a canticle spectrum smell
bending bow O gerundive air.

What can stand
forms anymore arranges a little

lower built motion
in dirt darling voice

chrome toroid
of who drawn back fauve elation

to then thing something out to
paint.

F

I often

know I

brighten but I

only emotes I

predict on or

I

cannot though enough of you

brave

internal sufferer

wield delicacy

out leg primary

arm

everything

tongue corner

beams

red something you

are off do I want what

passages do

to a certain

auspice

bird of oil

gravity aft

G

Make embarrassing difficult.
Psychoanalyses lock of orthodox type.
Knocks on a revery pattern interest.
Jacques all plural sine wave matter.
Some have image as mad prep.
Mountain objects to the rest of humbling.
Pronouns came and take math away.
Who has the rule in a ball game?
Naught nacht clambers up strum.
Presynaptic and postsynaptic operative.
NO reuptake a priori.
Oxygen Nylon Occident Nitrogen matrix weave.
Terrible hamper the schema toto wrong it.
Aphorism so much so eyes will have to end a window.
Like art of image directs a living bird whoot.
Pun oops a pneumonic see generation.
Anaphora is mush so hope words again again.
Polymerase across agar end to front transubstantiation.

H

Pun et panem
ludus and panem
ludus res publica

Magna Carta catapulta
boat a smile toy yes

boats and buoys

and what have you

milk and sugar

lipsmacking good milk and sugar
house the cap of a forsaken body

the thought retrieved
a little history

we call memory

but memory is a priority
not a generator

a priori is not a memory
nor a mechanical generator

a thought not
apophatic up to find

matter scurries off
nods and nodules loom

a body across feeling cylinder
a chime even

then never to know not to now
remember the shell

switch of apophatics to objects

and back remember a balloon or a popcorn

remember the state we got ourselves into
the order not able

to talk each other the flip to

switch so harried emotions arrange
variegated aesthetic

unknowledgeable as soul or word crap
out the stupid limosine tunnel

like some picture
an artist put there at the back

that scary what talks like retrieval
via suspicion

beauty changes
art and other recreations

and arrangements
of pain that fuck the neck

is the hot tag not a gene

dialogues precede and do not lead anywhere
but a wooded site no method

talks open
a foot or foot after foot feet or metric miles

knight to king
might have him flick a dog star and

dog ear driftwood

I

I know now why I go about
I now know a subject is
what holds for so long

stoop at the top to drop
a coin the dial absorbs

the jangle stuck a billfold
in plastic rectangles

the number flew up to bend mazes
in azimuth

a projective stunt
could forget rules

make me sad

though the flops of rules

register the mark toes make

the boat turn
a wake of the boat

the body a sound
receives as untrussed lingo

J

Cloud arranged
a styrene

pouf lush as a bell
or the personal

getting and remembering
are dirt and circle

hair of throat

forgetting and remembering
how to have a person check

and check out coy
glass smoke bird views

imaginary right to passage wave sine
Clark and Lewis

to parallax of scope top down to denature
protein as regarded as a page was

the Bible an octavo
preceded this looseness

blabs the page turns
the mulch of earth

arrogance a potato-plex

drive into kenning a logarithm
power shifts to subscript

cod liver oil lodge
back to your old home

your parents parent good persons

K

he spoke
you wheel

I am sorry our slurry
turns back as crisp

having no one to arrange
sun watches from that distance

that pull will be called warp in retrospect away
and thankful that that

thought could enboy luna

arm of blue coal-blown
fire does when I don't do

do skip down that miss
all camera and to turn

marriage circumnavigate
a livid blot

learn to tune
heart valve replacements

find it transpires
a shorter tongue train

L

Appropriate
such book dark isolates

the vocative hope
continues and do not sublimate

go solid to air

path contained a hugged heart
and the age of sound

thuno
knorat

accord by whom
words can drive out of the curve happiness

not arranged square ballast dunking
brown over

the crater the television lovingly tunes
to rustle over

land that clocks press me against is as

if I were dearth
to the way out to the loring

aware a crown type to match
a man it stands

to harangue a fandango

marvel nomenclature-derived plenitude
could only create

more than to make it swell
as a sphere

loose clod

and the spills of that

small air clod and configure
shelf and remember that bandwidth

to go away as parity
can take it apart along

navigator

nap   blip
        house

atonal measure contorts a cantata
out of a melba

deft strife to push hubris to act
against what fifty days

at iliam
against a maker

tanks the test to diagonal emotion

across the rectangle

M

Sovereign clam
loosen ataxia

a hand slipped around
the clink of the arcs is
a chink in a door

stole off the lip flax
the funnel hat collides

and continue onto candid glance

harp on hold
a ton drawn
nouns spring to form

flower directly a logical nature
grown through

river continuance of that wheeling
bird flew off

apart from time to ripple circumstantials

that to say
get away from it asshole apparently

that is why I

coal mine order up doom all a

vein out for balance and slight bend

to feel out balance that
Earl of Gloucester knew what

coal blue
coal-blown

fire does

pucker or

contract a separate

virus over orange
a sty ajar no

mystery nor majestry

talk open
common courtesy

sorry stove door hook
convention

next fall crimson bone forks
and chlorophyll webbings pile

a remonstrance
a season rakes under trees

scares the Dickens out

of us a trick a parlor ascertains
pieces languishing

a stanza leaves and cannot contain
the sweet organ year if livers fall

a lobotomy of logos

over there coughing
up pins and lipid strands…

count them biologies…

real joys…

of acceptance…

N

Sibilant toward
possibility a bigger river

bottom description
takes silt toward a lock crack

level land reclaims
then the inner source

to whom
it rinses as fortification

to drive
a lock to live and flounces

little bend and a little bond
a latter clank

and the listless know

the spatula function
not to contain

never to known
now throne show

an even light beam
a bounding kitchen

and to no one
ever to clown

low of open
épée

a fertile third against a bay

never around
a location

never around

a roll of fabric

print never known

no more

lather behind books

shelve knowledge

though infertile units and standard

O

an alabaster
candelabra

favor four or five
times center

narrowing mecatum
anglepoint

recognize nobis

sorry wrong palm
tree out my head
sorry

so long

liker
finger

ladder
climber
oof

fade
to print so

now

fake
a core

P

open onto hand

onto silver
out to the self
self Viennese
flotsam the mirror
ball pixel pop
optic ectopic

proud onto street
revise ends recur

no horrible
or no relic of

nasty number
ram side le mountain
caught to catch up

ghost that ole figura emotional
remember that one that we talked about

remember that movie talked about
foundering on the arrival of door burl
so clam have shape

no no bounds
caul fall fowl fallow

motor clue back

shantih me a person
al bribe la burrow
a skein alive
mechanistic fern coil
onto toxic Radha shine

believe all smiles are rainbows or
Latin can tax

Q

Single proclaim
sample
struts run new
drop
hold onto leg

leg around
and up to the blue
circle in porcelain
clean
to mark

check a gold
sign a diamond
think about

pine twinkle
stand or bark

arma virumque
Destin Desitin
faith ear

like imagined lack
a droop jetsam

jetsam stream sound
like big ocean

gulf nether
he flocks
the turn of bird day turns
morsed to that relative reason

familiar cloverleaf
functions as recognizable
symbol dairy
encompassing a trapezoid

Barney in a doctrine

type against familial
recognizance in that

self-region
long to enter zones built
dogs will enter
as mysteriously

a violet plastic nether
to consider ozone
triangle arrives to

discovery the brain

turn of magnitude to promise
because subs and lasagna are delicious

R

take what you can
screen what you can

can you derive
Shop-Rite got the can-can

admit impediments host
melt on tongue

diagram a sentence
person on person a

hard trick
the rivulets proceed

dust upon dust   upon door
red udon

shift instruction

poles connect and entail

talk between a spoon
a bowl inside bowling

rev ten green than yellow

glass heats year inside decade
inside one hundred

stick picture in dirt
exit the swan
cower down skid landscape
eddy on an egg

S

All that
got called sir today
by someone
today older than me

all that has
been can
go round cylinders

to
string out of troubles

blared out that can

a little
covered nylon pulls out down

the ladder spiders sidewind
longed for bird

to hand
the hand it takes

to out
never a climb bland

arm to arrow toward
a muffle twitch

I can see
now that I

can Charleston and coast
Wheeling a triangle

New York
on back map all time

it takes to true
releases never

mind the threat
of a continual

voicer in a throat
never smile away

the body

hold its hand
hold an arm

things change
hold an arm

things change
as dimes fly

over the center of aqua anterior face

gram air down

aardvark
egg toward land

twine shapes to come back

take a train

past the grey
door seared and
continued on down

the chunk of the car
cameras along
unsubstantial it is static

function as a remainder
of time to go on

to else wave
cabled derivative

and oblivious to curve

an integral
sign the non-form
containing the loose

beaver dam
moved from difficulty and memory
sediment and grade

mouth an aisle

that prime
house irrational
number calls froth a mama

T

Harboring a recon
Harpes a bergher

hoop a boa Malay to a claim

maraud a container

continue the farthing

map sing along dander
scarf about the nicer

loose elation undulate

what crystal doxology
led brake leg nor lasso cor-mat-ik

two to tram it
up on

who to have
to go on

mark the mark
or on no

summer salt
the sweat has

lifted it
to croup the

no no
having had it

U

On town that way
to swim together

ands hold
along outside it
and to hold

a part of an ear
corn delivered obviously from a field
and plate dribblings.

I can all I want
I who want all I can cancel.

From the get-go the modern
byword has been reduction.

Right? Shunt for brain
have an image for a dollar.

A geneology of morals
is just a cascade of aesthetics

that how it operates as retrospective
deciduously would not answer.

I would rather cliché act one critique.
I would rather create but customize.

V

On a bus a man
flirted with a woman
and a man
concomitantly as a truck
pulled ahead and braked
with TOM CAT on the side plus
the picture of the cat and
tail a sentimental tail.

W

Objects fall as easy risers.

So what that
I don't want the earth

quick to jack
the aroma or jamb the center

sound to round
the scope dark funnel

cake addenda have more
relationship

the lopped sector
a hip a planet calls up to drop in

lopped because its key contains
ideas meant

plashed little curve clouted
onto and seems

a handy crown crowd
clods transistors

that draw meaning down against the culture of metaphor
bacteria so to say vector it is to

male it bad
male mitochondria

a lipid swabs   a wafted cross   the dream cell.

X

The bridge a bridge
and island island

heave to have
reservation about looking ahead
not so

bad to say
that commendable OK
who doesn't
want this but faith
or sees this but
yelps to get there

or it
no want to weave
or to make

a hewn

arranger of dots
square air

who?
What wants that square meal
and staunch

the fuck of invert
we hear

to there first
because somebody
had a dam
and melted the back of a car

firmness of that
thought I engulfed

whole stems rose
and stamp on

that is what
flat you see to
pitch of anger
pissed to
name in prefect katakana

the dream I encircle
because I hop the ensemble
to say
both doors open say

Bakhtin the skull
structure drug ouch

Y

There has been
too much left about

to think
infinitely better

hated residue or the hammy constrict

has lied its last lay

or dumped its club

planaria doubt scoot
memory toward nutrition

and love hey
little arranger

wheretofore this talk

to how it can describe

outside what sight has

because strong images
of death have real counterparts

so a material
not so much occulted

as not so much as it is a material

to correspond to something
we can have inside us
since we're conditioned

against the sense
of what makes
true heart the note
to have

so long
the dole

you crave
oh-oh
remember this type of thing

you think hallmark
makes the john
swirl brighter

me no

can do

zip blind
yeah me an equator what belief

has a foot
on to on pick it

what choice do I have is
what everybody says.

Certain
methods of survival

get the drift
that opened skyward there

to keep
real and elide
the flake combed stars the

little meter
separates a little strain

to train
each type a word

can clog. Use as much
a link to derivation.

Blessed out of pressure
and confused meaning torture

to say the balance struck in a zone
can leaf or bring a land on

a jetty slips or the milk
of what that

sunset must
mean to make the beautiful.

I never want to have
to make the broken experience.

Let's have Italian heros
for lunch the horizon says.

Z

This is what to say to
though who would buy it

tired I track a plundered ground
cool to dunk down a sandwich

a sponge to open mouth
to it drops and pulses out of

the loose a crisp nature
accoutrement to film still

and the balance of your eyes
because they now are necessary

to me everything proceeds
form the father

the son

confusing the difference how

to break the knock
that locks logic though to the

less flat that proclaim soon a bump

on a surface as sense
of all press us.

God, I   think it just   finishes itself.

Born in 1973, Tom Kraft grew up outside Bridgeton, New Jersey. After receiving a B.A. from the University of Virginia in 1996, Kraft moved to New York City, where he wrote *The Type a Thing.* He recently moved back to Charlottesville and enjoys its surrounding beauty.